Clothes
Around the World

Clare Lewis

Raintree is an imprint of Capstone Global Library Limited, a company incorporated in England and Wales having its registered office at 7 Pilgrim Street, London, EC4V 6LB – Registered company number: 6695582

www.raintreepublishers.co.uk
myorders@raintreepublishers.co.uk

Text © Capstone Global Library Limited 2015
Paperback edition first published in 2015
The moral rights of the proprietor have been asserted.

Edited by Joanna Issa, Shelly Lyons, Diyan Leake and Helen Cox Cannons
Designed by Cynthia Akiyoshi
Original illustrations © Capstone Global Library Ltd 2014
Picture research by Elizabeth Alexander and Tracy Cummins
Production by Victoria Fitzgerald
Originated by Capstone Global Library Ltd
Printed and bound in China

ISBN 978 1 406 28201 6 (hardback)
18 17 16 15 14
10 9 8 7 6 5 4 3 2 1

ISBN 978 1 406 28208 5 (paperback)
19 18 17 16 15
10 9 8 7 6 5 4 3 2 1

British Library Cataloguing in Publication Data
A full catalogue record for this book is available from the British Library.

Acknowledgements
We would like to thank the following for permission to reproduce photographs: Alamy pp. 8 & 22a (both © Horizons WWP), 12 & 22d (both © Hemis), 16 (© Ian Shaw), 23b (© Hemis), 23c (© Ian Shaw); Corbis pp. 17 & 23a (both © Ocean), 21 (© Sean De Burca); Getty Images pp. 4 (Adam Hester), 11 (Ariel Skelley), 13 & 22b (both LEON NEAL/AFP); Shutterstock pp. 1 (© 41), 2 (© Worldpics), 3 (© watin), 6 & 22c (both © Sofarina79), 7 (© Zoran Karapancev), 10 (© tankist276), 14 (© Tatiana Morozova), 15 & 22c (both © df028), 24 (© Worldpics); Superstock pp. 5 (allindiaimages), 9 (age footstock), 18 (Juice Images), 19 (Stefan Kiefer/imageb /imagebroker.net), 20 (Design Pics).

Front cover photograph of a young girl performing in a folk dance show in the Zocalo in Oaxaca City, Mexico, reproduced with permission of Getty Images (Politzer/Lonely Planet Images). Back cover photograph of a boy dressed up for a Hindu festival in Malaysia reproduced with permission of Alamy (© Hemis).

Contents

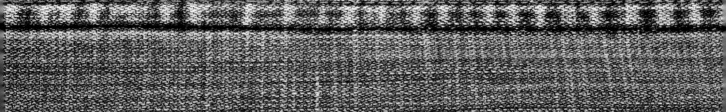

Clothes everywhere

All around the world, people wear clothes.

People wear different types of clothes.

Some clothes are very colourful.

Some clothes make us look smart.

Why do people wear clothes?

Some clothes keep us warm.

Some clothes help to keep us cool.

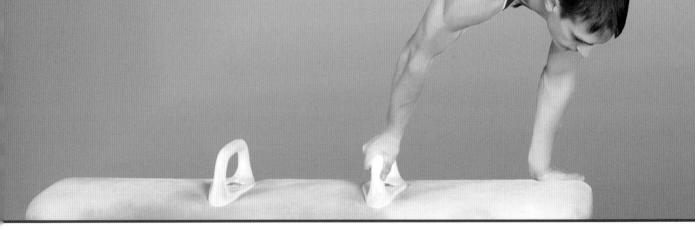

Some clothes are good for sport.

Some clothes are good for work.

People wear special clothes for festivals.

Sometimes special clothes show that a person is important.

Some clothes are good for a
wedding.

Some clothes are good for dancing.

Sometimes we wear uniforms.

Sometimes we wear dressing-up clothes for fun.

Where do people get their clothes?

Some people make their own clothes.

Some people buy their clothes.

People wear clothes everywhere.

What do you like to wear?

Map of clothes around the world

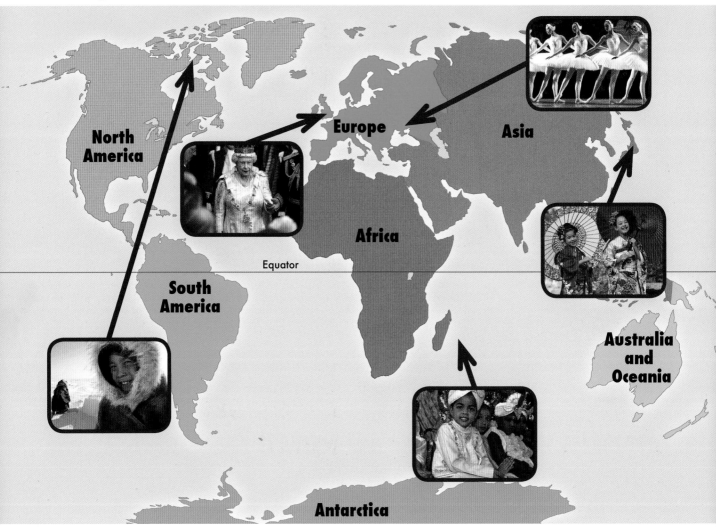

Picture glossary

dressing-up clothes
clothes people wear to look like someone or something else

festival special time for a group of people

uniform clothes that are all the same

23

Index

Notes for parents and teachers

Before reading

Show children a globe and explain that it is a model of Earth. Discuss how people live all over the world and identify the seven continents, including the continent on which you live. Ask children to think about what they are wearing. When they got dressed, did they think about the weather? Why did they choose to wear what they are wearing? Discuss how people in the community wear many different types of clothes, as well as people all over the world.

After reading

- Turn to page 16 and re-read the text. Ask children to define *uniform*. Discuss how the photo illustrates uniforms and have children name other types of uniform.

- Point out the map on page 22. Explain that this map is a flat representation of the globe. Demonstrate for children how to use the map to identify the continents on which different photos from the book were taken.